Working Horses

Christine Butterworth and Donna Bailey

MACMILLAN EDUCATION

This horse is a show jumper.
It jumps round the ring over
very high fences.

These are racehorses.

They gallop fast around the track.

Some horses pull light carts when
they race around the track.

Working horses also pull carts.

This big horse is pulling
a cart full of hay.

Sometimes the Queen uses her horses
to pull her carriage.

Some horses work on farms.
They help plough the fields.

8

In some countries the roads are
too steep for cars and trucks.
Then people use pack horses
to help carry things.

These boys look after sheep.
They live in the mountains.
Their horses help them
to round up the sheep.

10

Cowboys use horses on their ranches
to round up the cattle.

At rodeos cowboys try
to ride wild horses.

The wild horses buck and try to throw the cowboys off.

The cowboys tame the wild horses.
Then they are safe to ride.

These horses are too small to ride.
They are the smallest horses
in the world.

Index

cart racing 4
cowboys 11, 12, 13, 14
farm horses 5, 6, 8
herding 10, 11

pack horses 9
ploughing 8
Queen's horses 7
racehorses 3

riding 12, 14, 15
rodeos 12
show jumping 2
wild horses 12, 13, 14